Everyone I Don't Like Is Hitler

I Child's Guide to Political Discussion

GenesiusTimes.com

Copyright © 2025 by Genesius Times. All Rights Reserved. Printed in the United States of America.

This book was produced by Genesius Times, GenesiusTimes.com
ISBN Paperback: 978-1-60020-156-1 Ebook: 978-1-60020-157-8

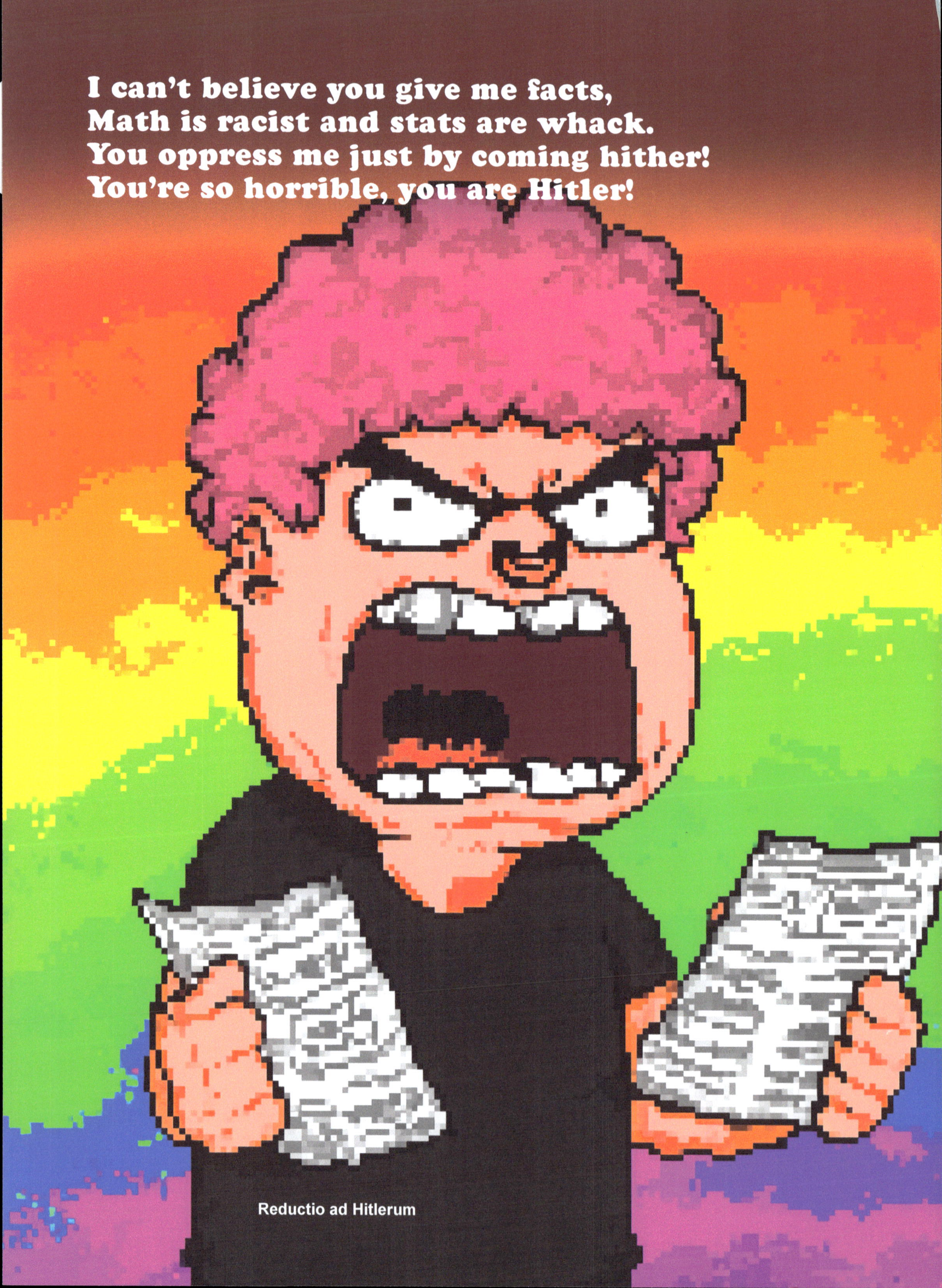
I can't believe you give me facts,
Math is racist and stats are whack.
You oppress me just by coming hither!
You're so horrible, you are Hitler!
Reductio ad Hitlerum

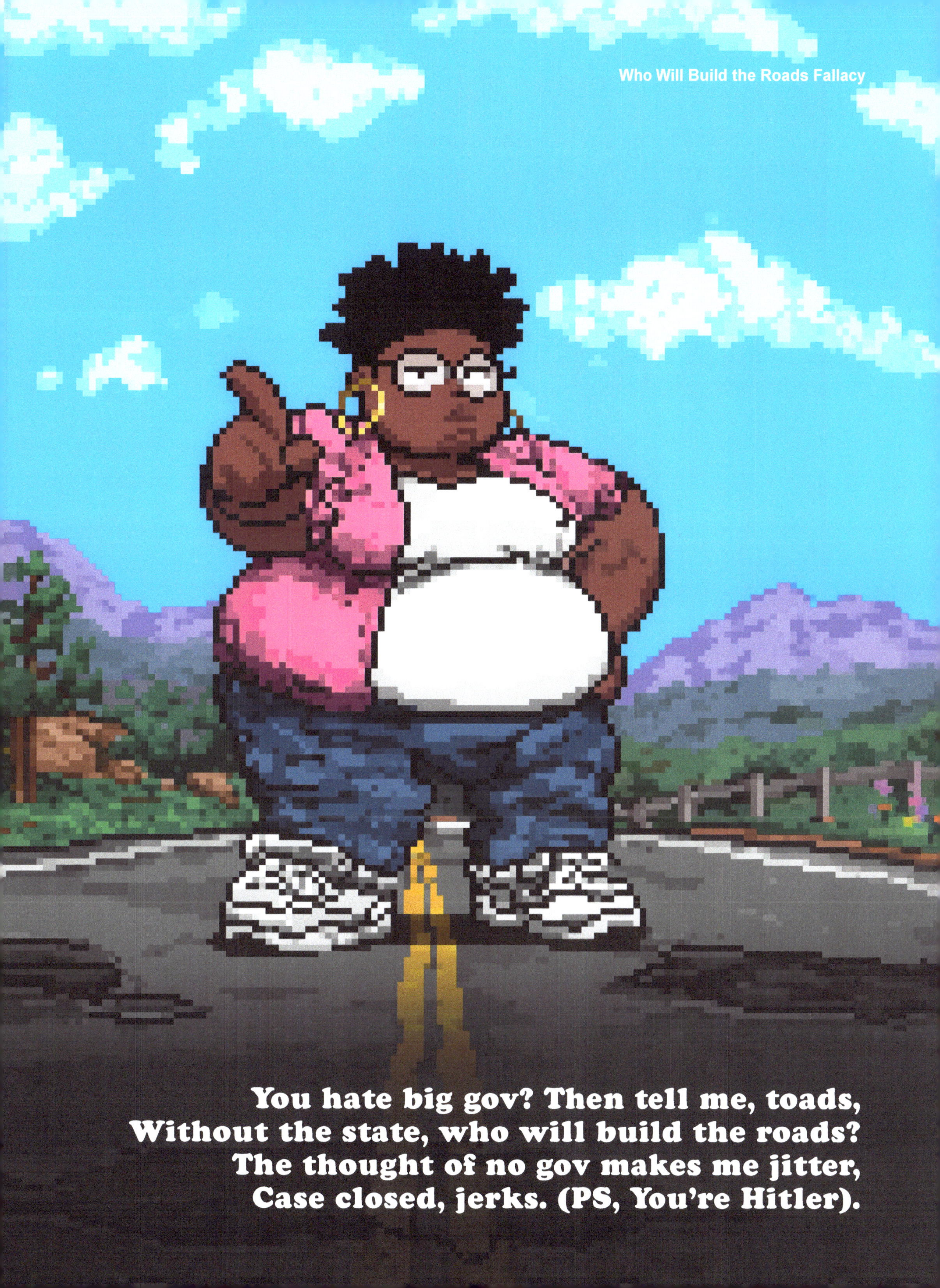
Who Will Build the Roads Fallacy
You hate big gov? Then tell me, toads,
Without the state, who will build the roads?
The thought of no gov makes me jitter,
Case closed, jerks. (PS, You're Hitler).

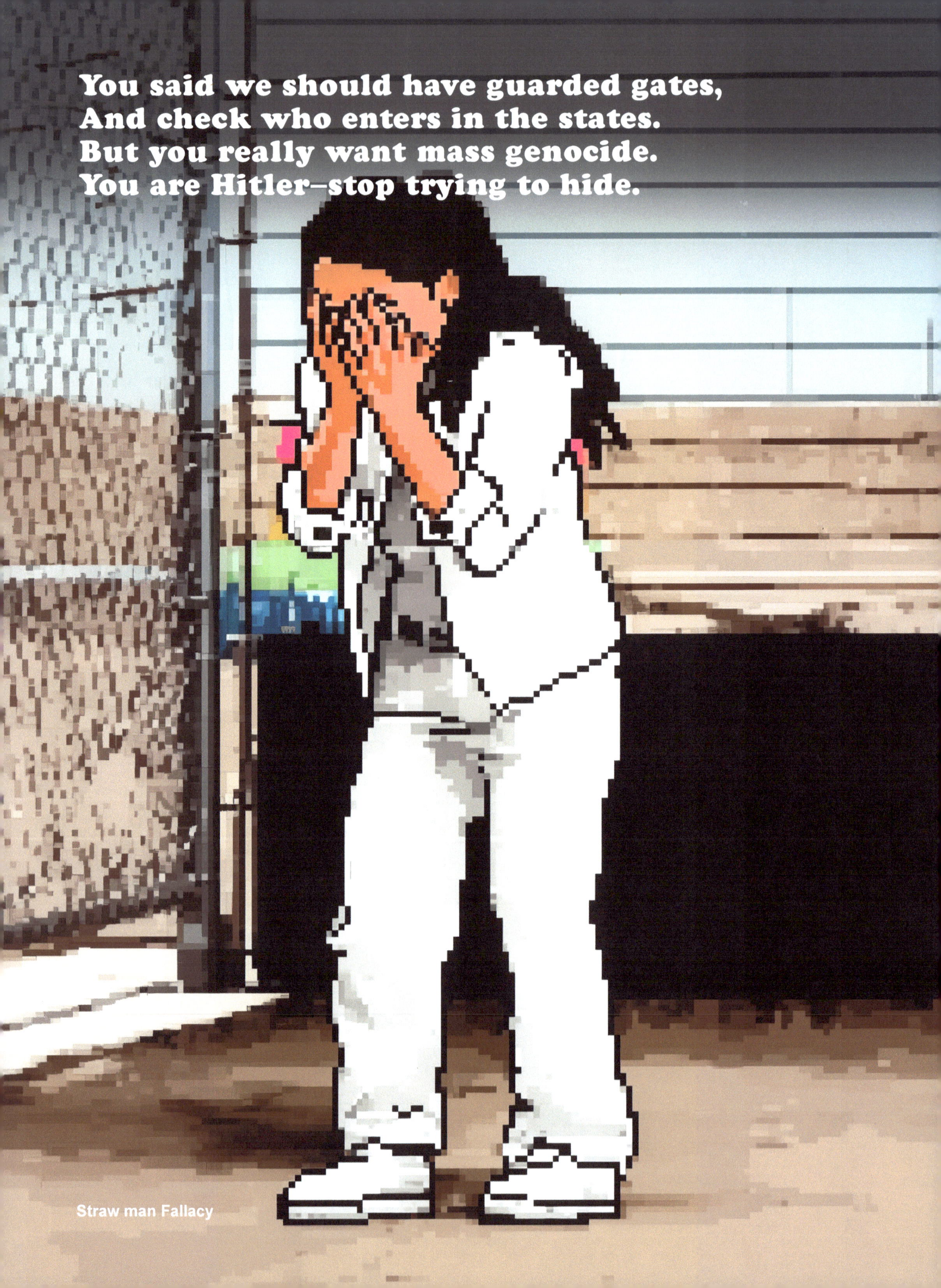

You said we should have guarded gates,
And check who enters in the states.
But you really want mass genocide.
You are Hitler–stop trying to hide.

Straw man Fallacy

The polls are clear, I read the news,
Everyone agrees with my great views.
Consensus proves my logic's fitter,
Deny it once, and boom – you're Hitler.

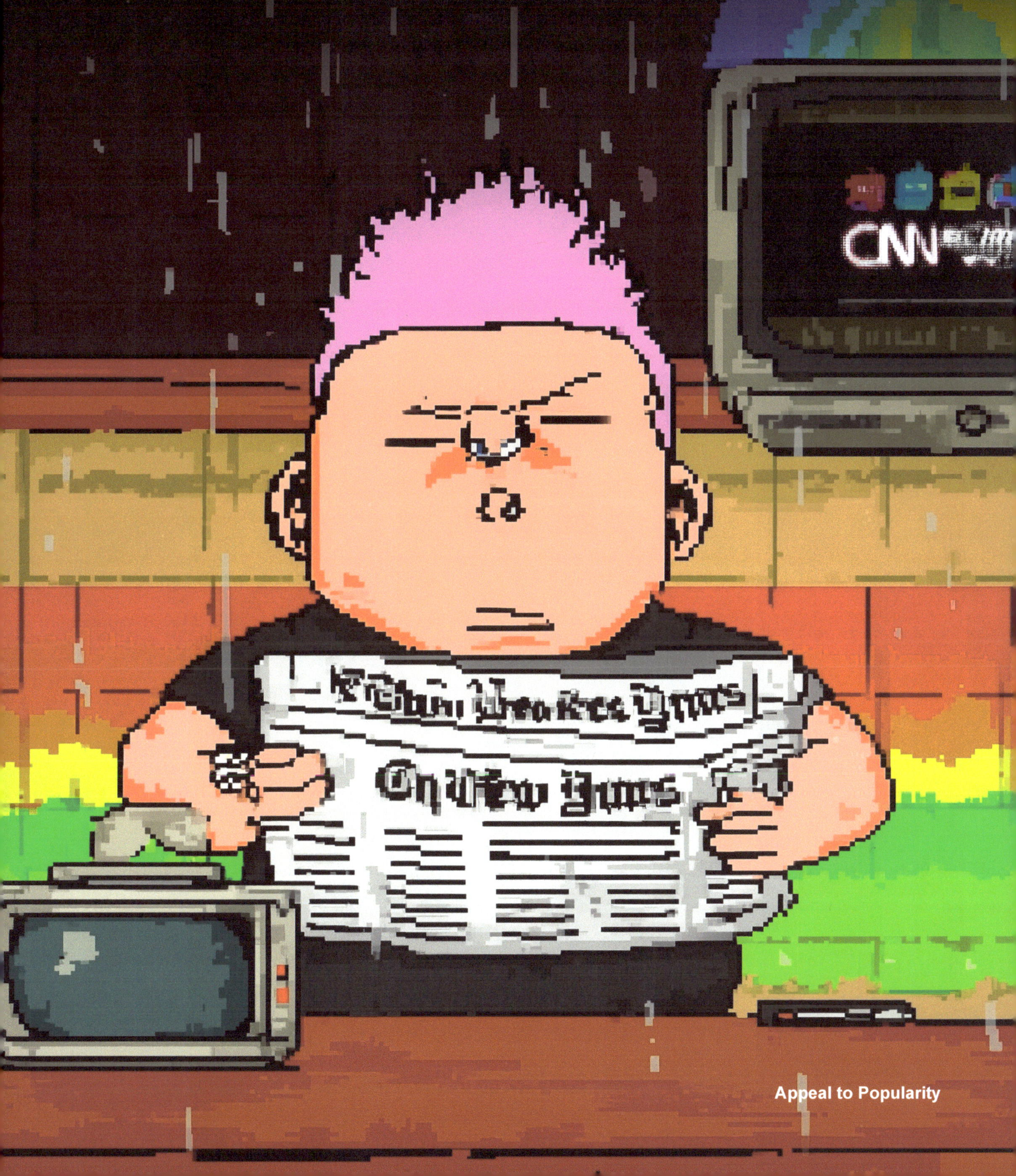
CNN

Appeal to Popularity

I moved the goalposts, can't you tell?
First it was one point, now it's twelve.
Find a source that passes my filter!
Scoreboard says that you are Hitler.

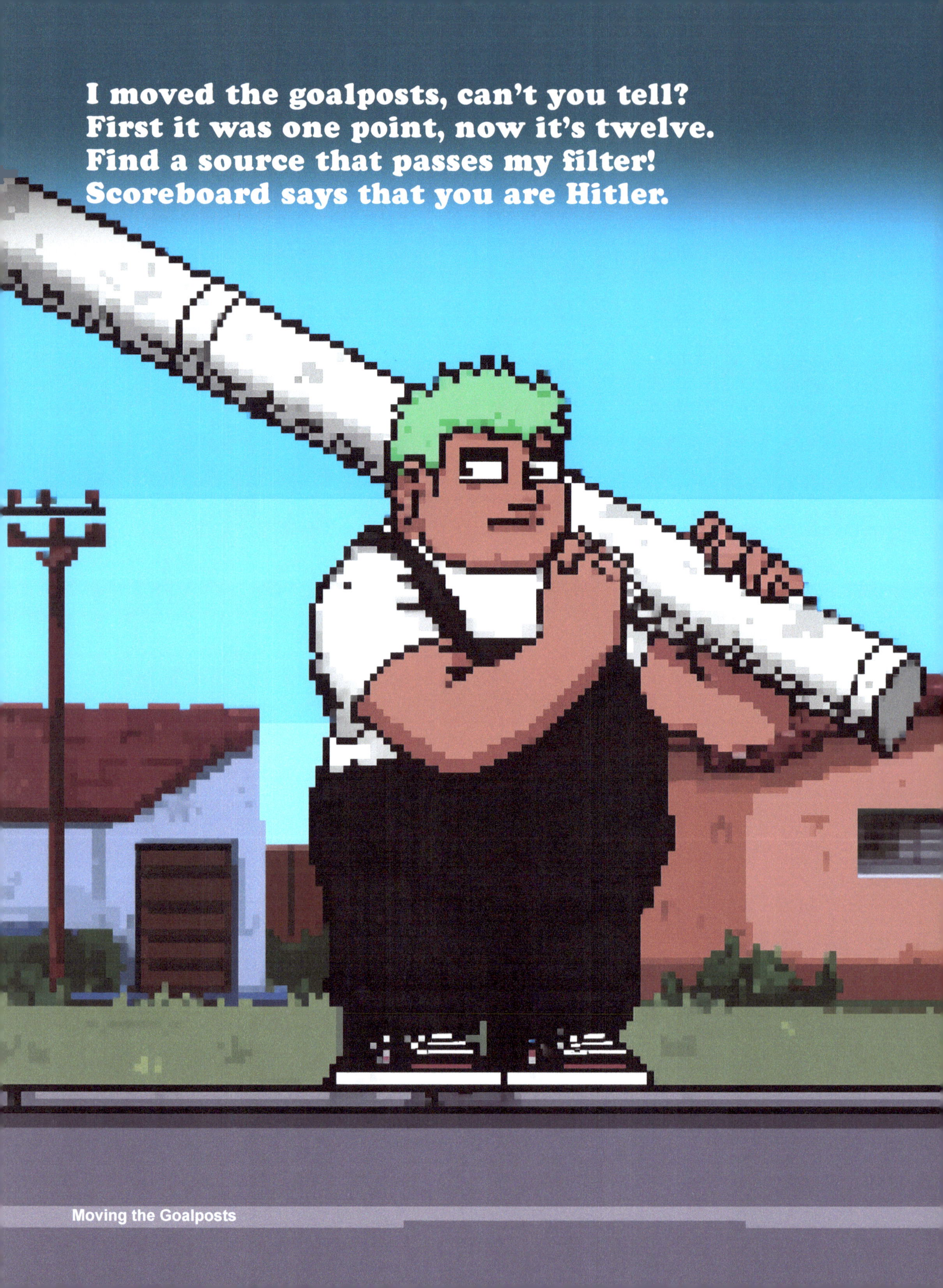

Moving the Goalposts

Don't question me, don't be uncouth,
'Cause Dr. Fauci speaks the truth.
His lab coat trumps you sneezy spitter.–
Disagree with him, and you're Hitler.

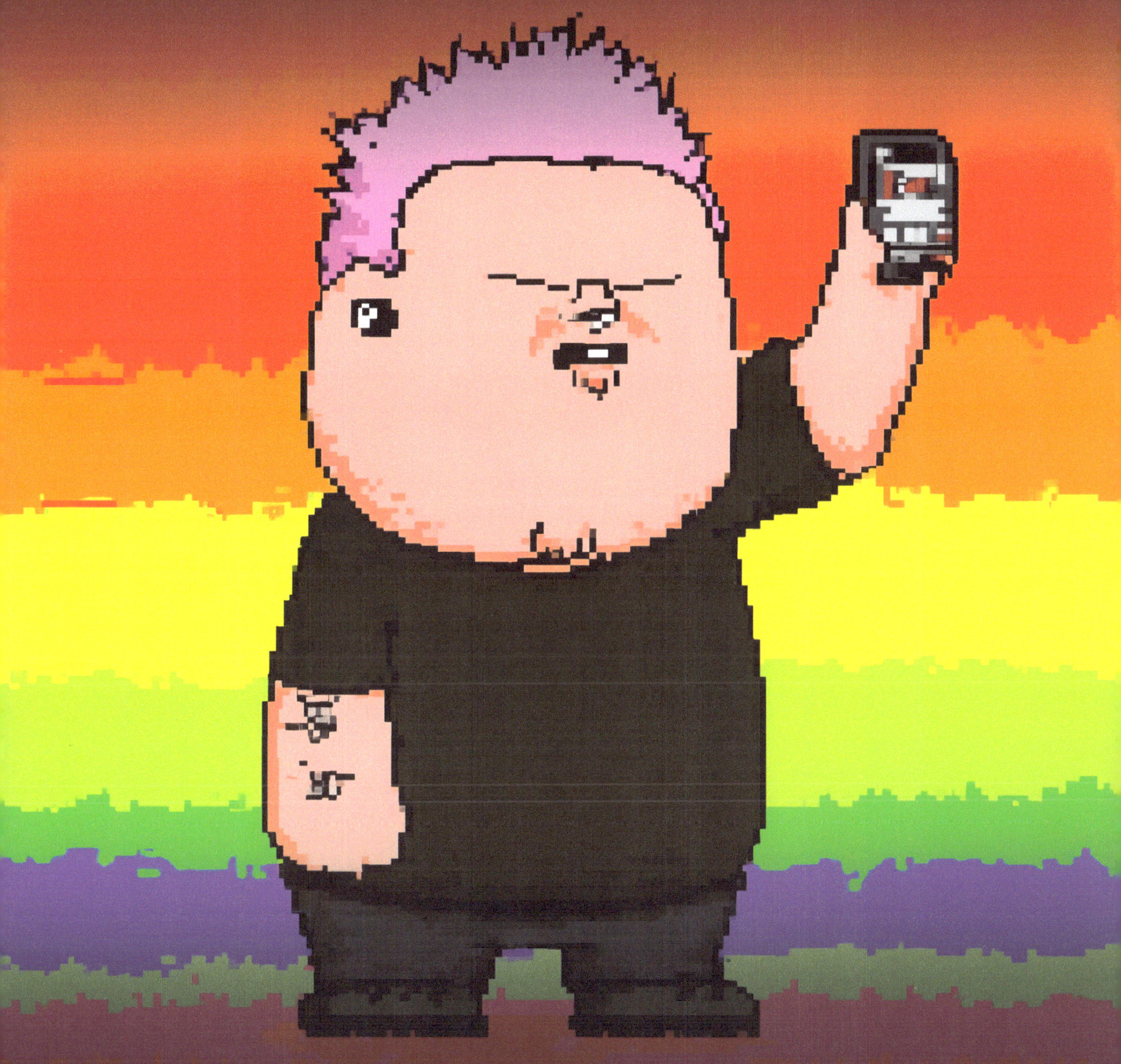

Appeal to Authority

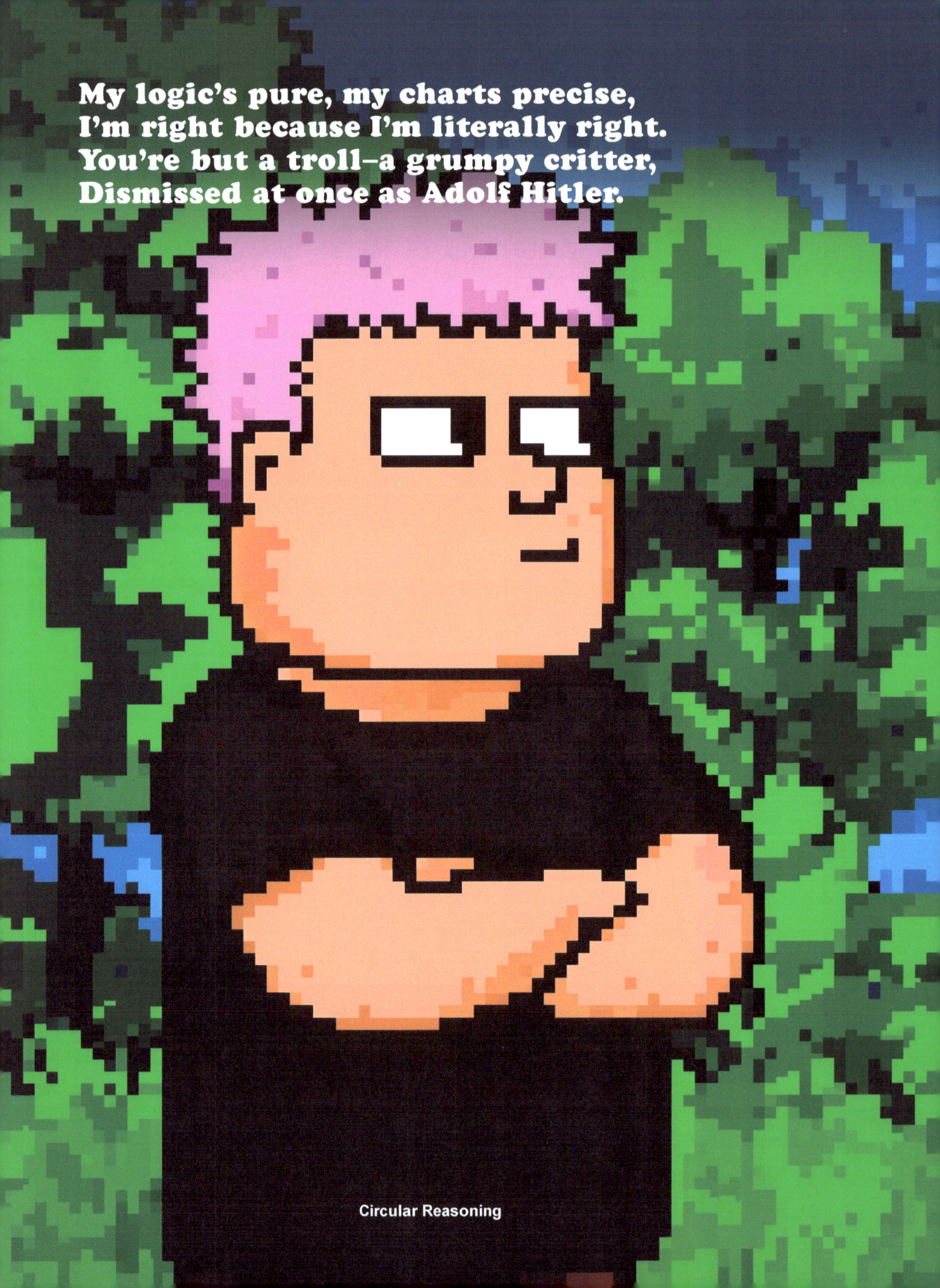
My logic's pure, my charts precise,
I'm right because I'm literally right.
You're but a troll–a grumpy critter,
Dismissed at once as Adolf Hitler.

Circular Reasoning

Broken Window Fallacy

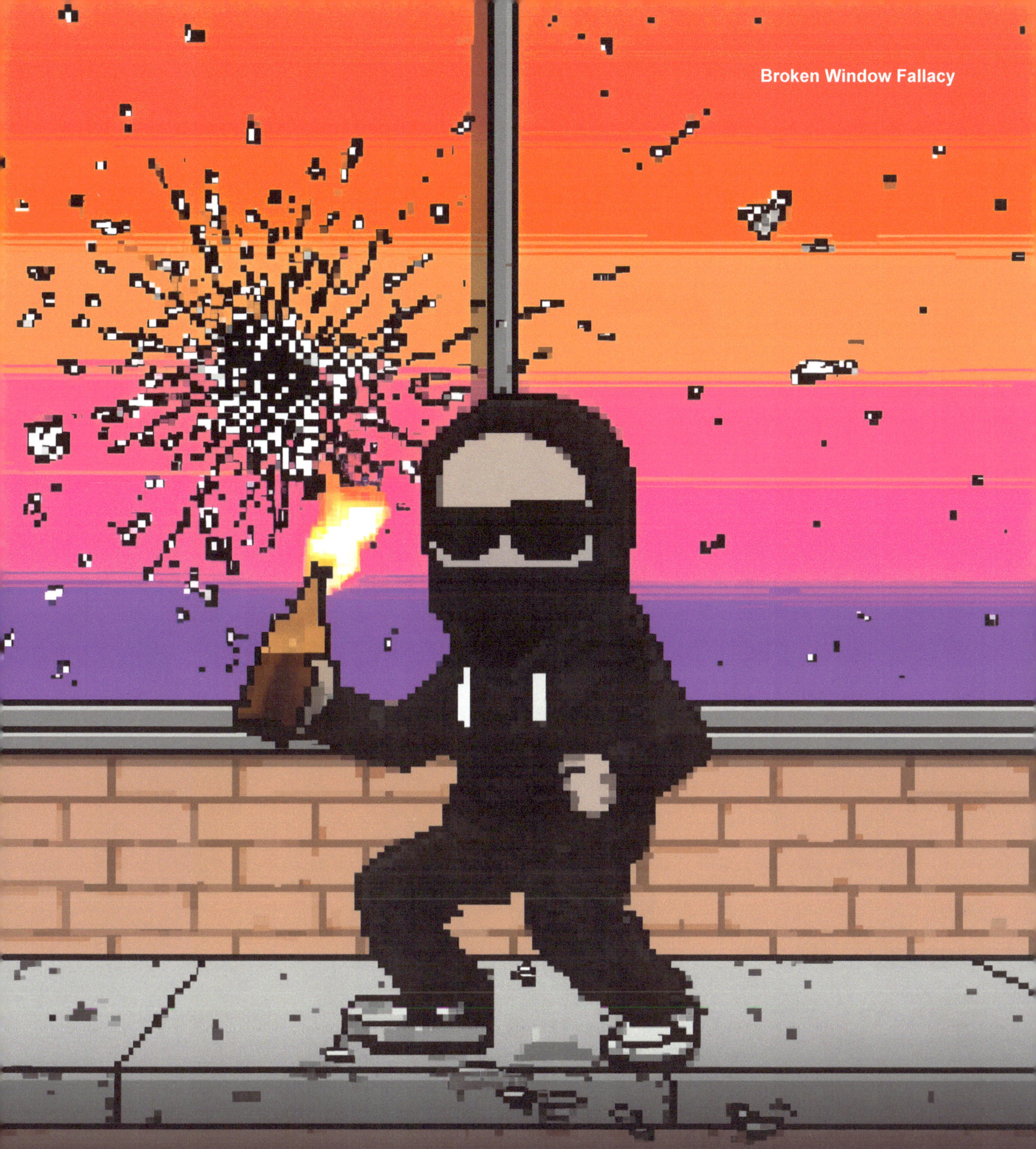

Smash the shops, it's good, you see,
Creates new jobs for glass debris.
The wrecking ball makes all this glitter.
Don't question that you little Hitler!

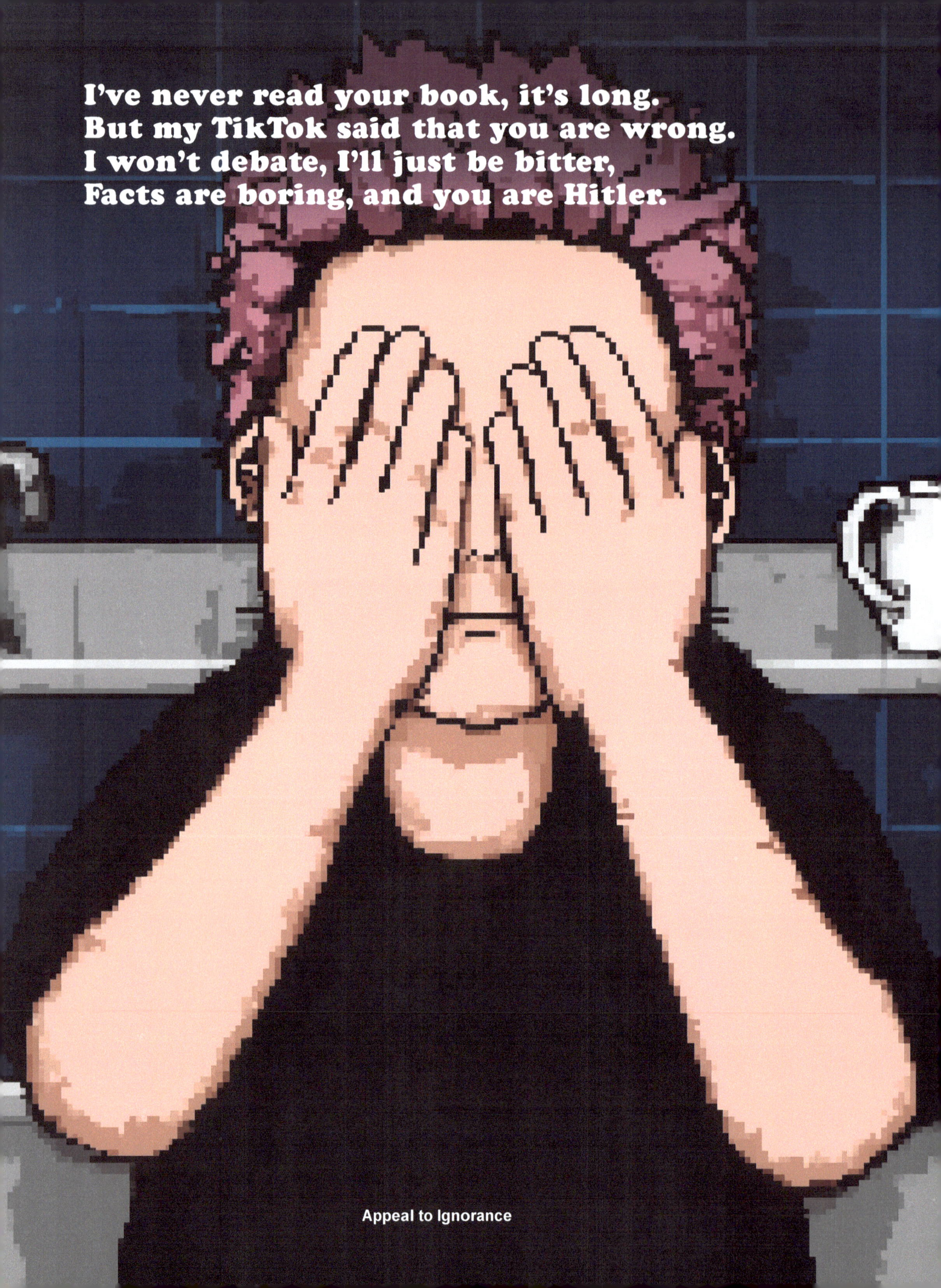
I've never read your book, it's long.
But my TikTok said that you are wrong.
I won't debate, I'll just be bitter,
Facts are boring, and you are Hitler.

Appeal to Ignorance

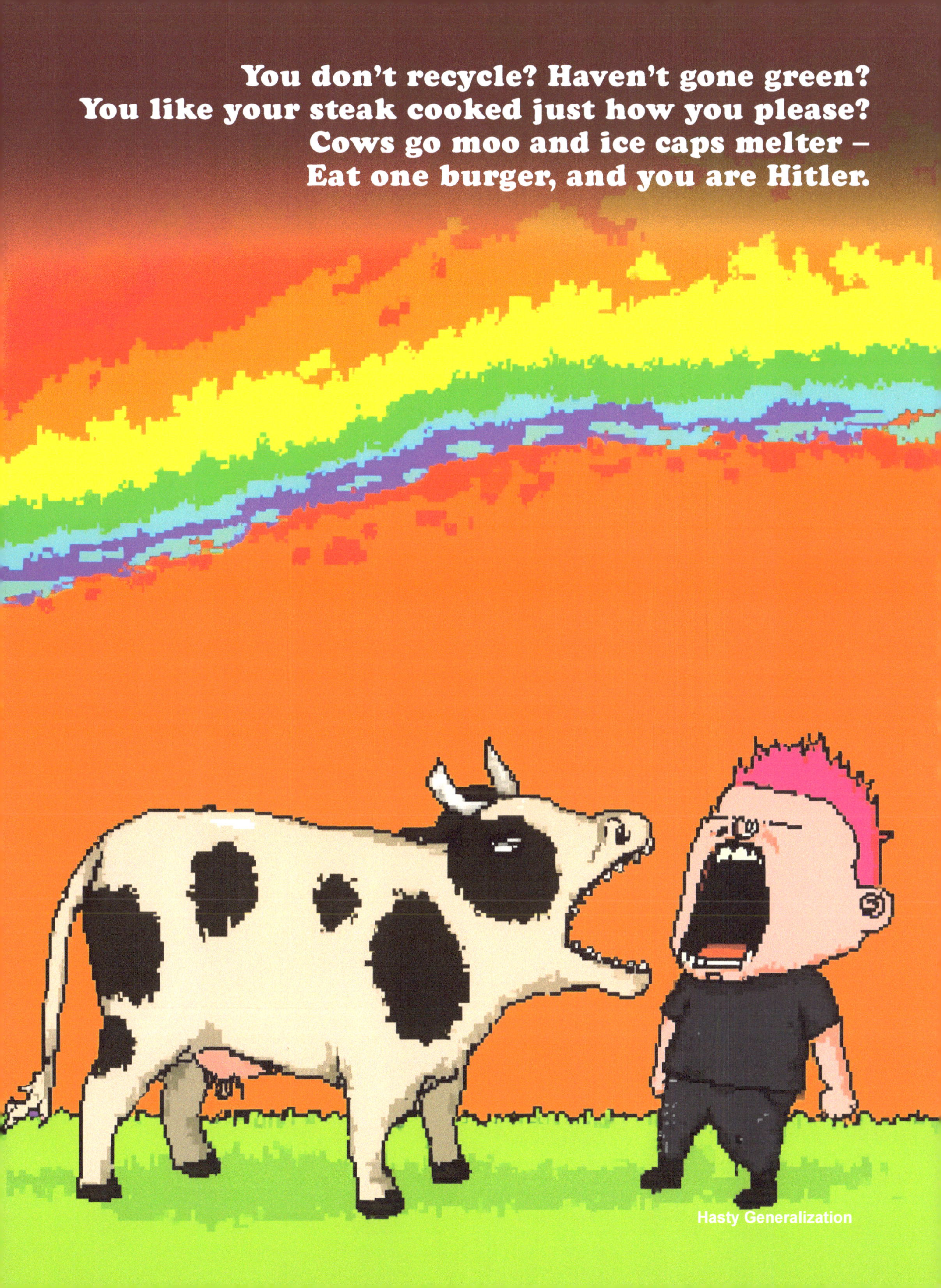
You don't recycle? Haven't gone green?
You like your steak cooked just how you please?
Cows go moo and ice caps melter –
Eat one burger, and you are Hitler.
Hasty Generalization

Ad Hominem/Appeal to Authority

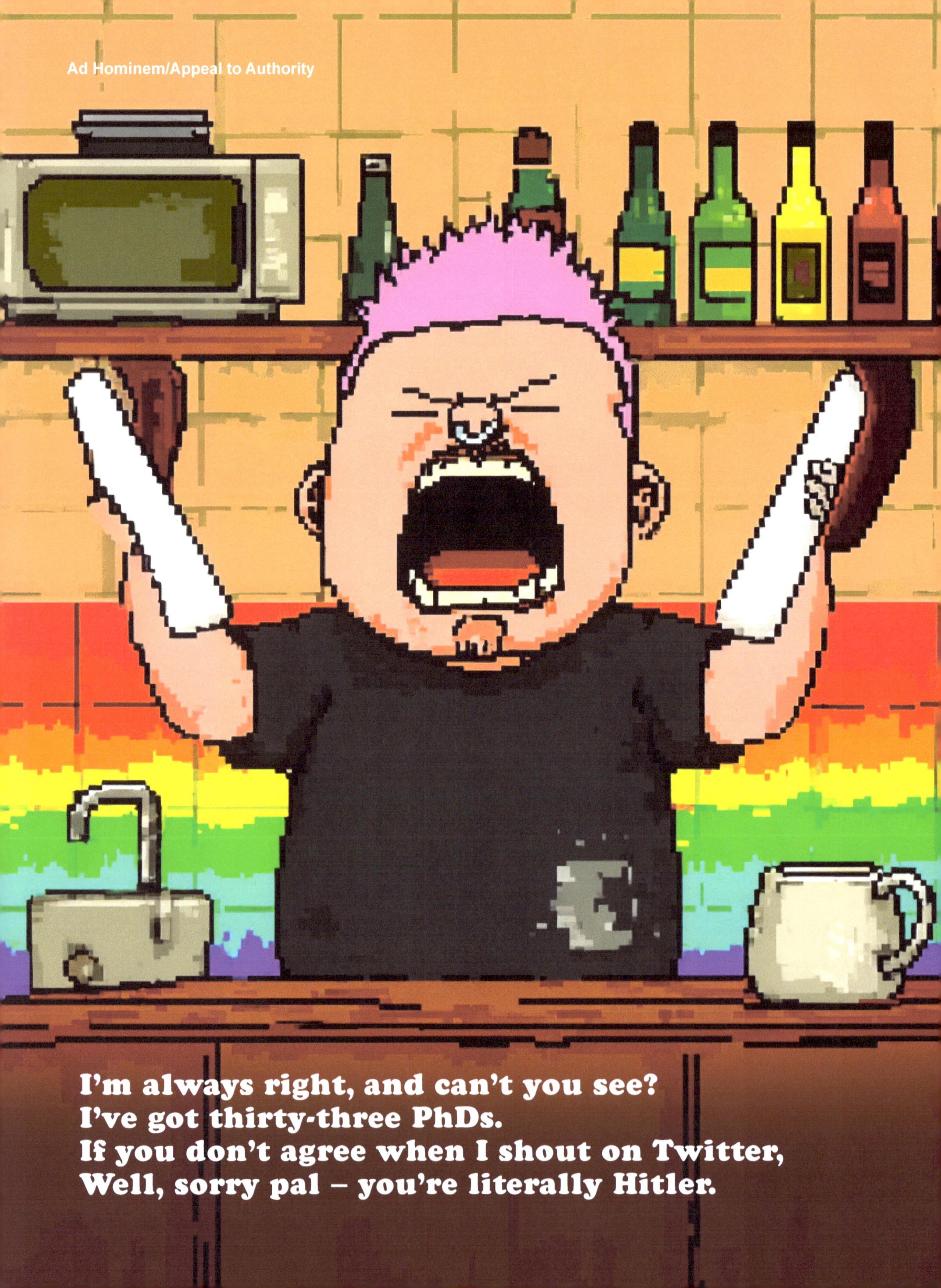

I'm always right, and can't you see?
I've got thirty-three PhDs.
If you don't agree when I shout on Twitter,
Well, sorry pal – you're literally Hitler.

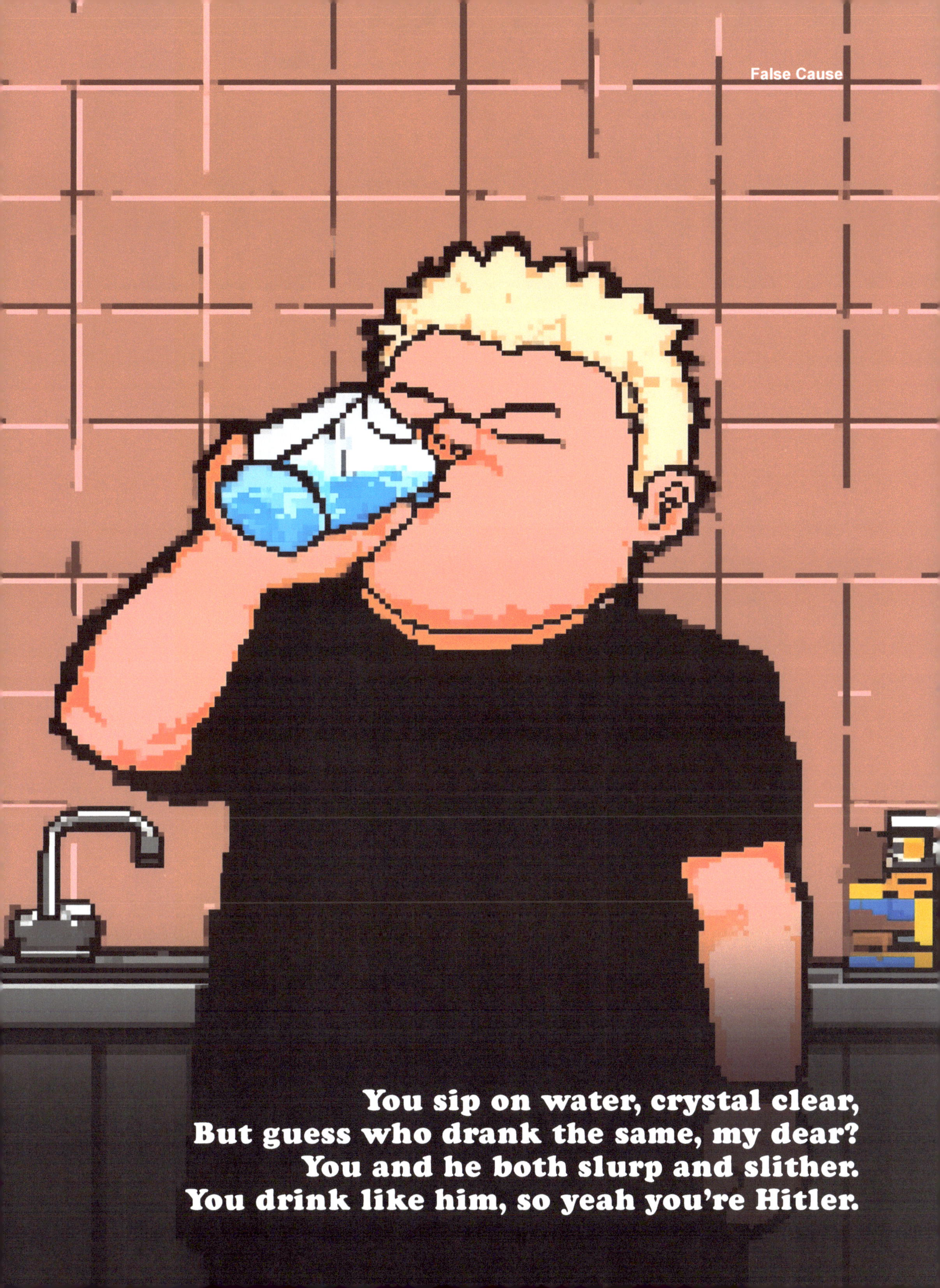
You sip on water, crystal clear,
But guess who drank the same, my dear?
You and he both slurp and slither.
You drink like him, so yeah you're Hitler.

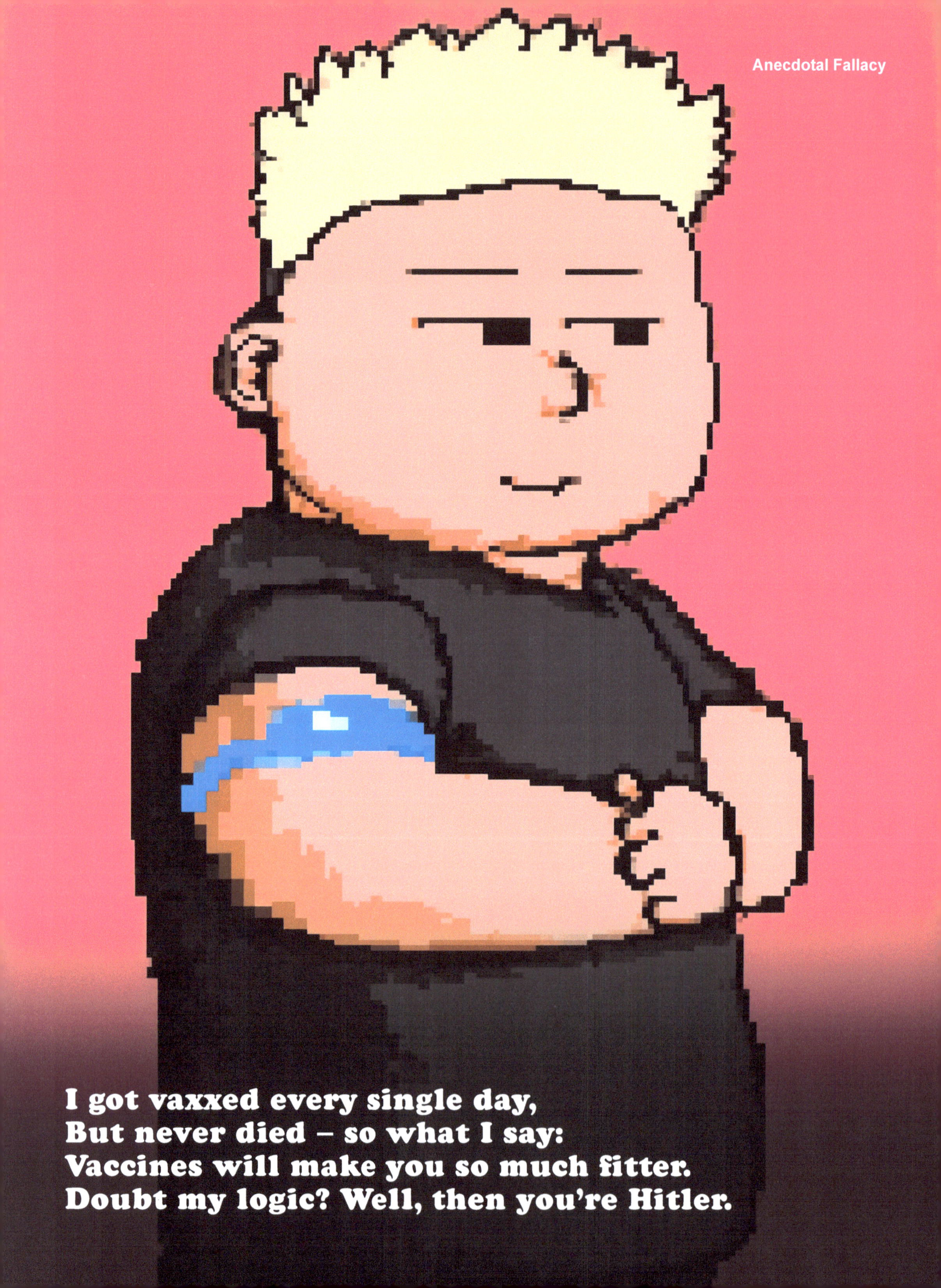
Anecdotal Fallacy
I got vaxxed every single day,
But never died – so what I say:
Vaccines will make you so much fitter.
Doubt my logic? Well, then you're Hitler.

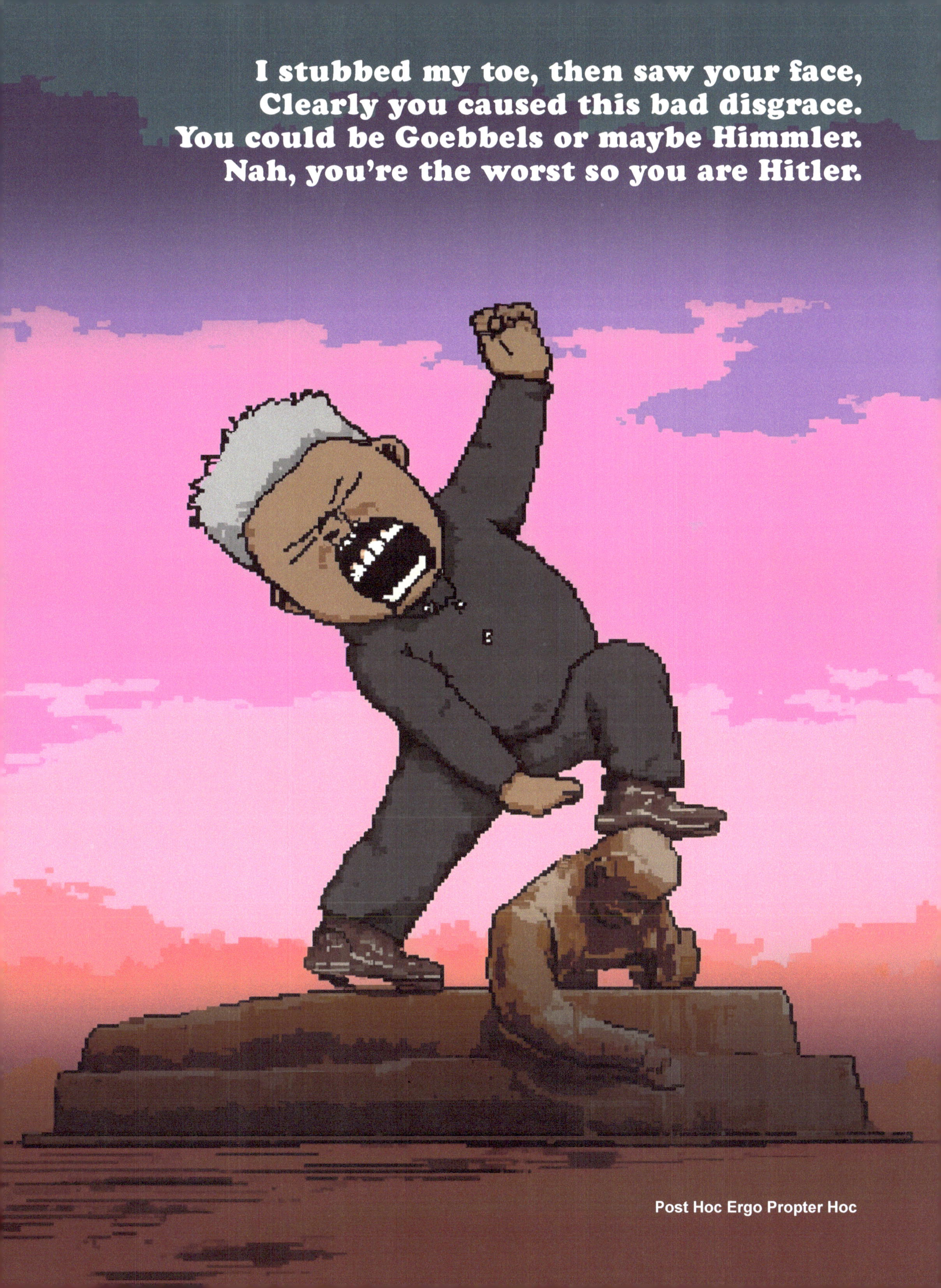
I stubbed my toe, then saw your face,
Clearly you caused this bad disgrace.
You could be Goebbels or maybe Himmler.
Nah, you're the worst so you are Hitler.
Post Hoc Ergo Propter Hoc

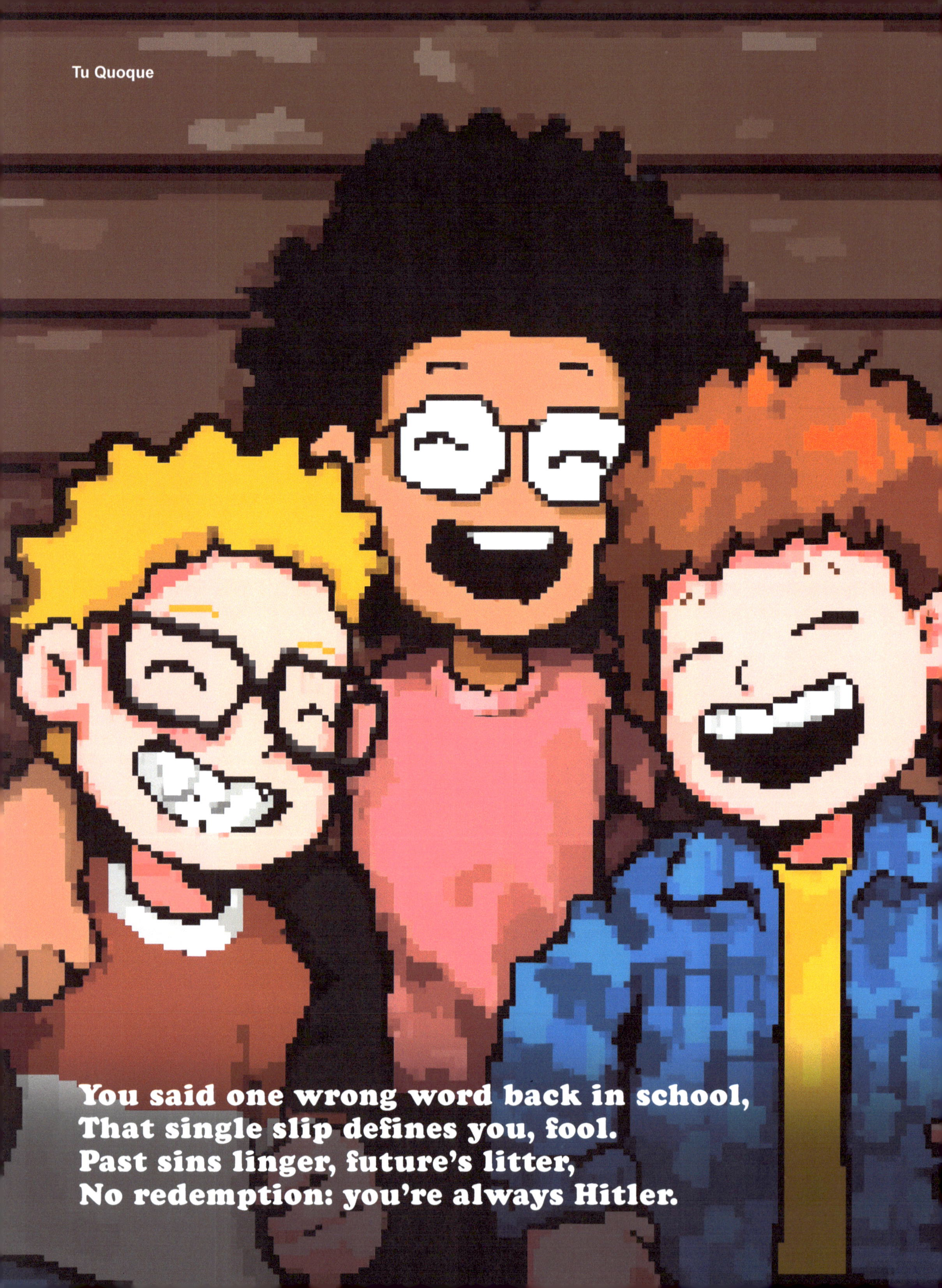

You said one wrong word back in school,
That single slip defines you, fool.
Past sins linger, future's litter,
No redemption: you're always Hitler.

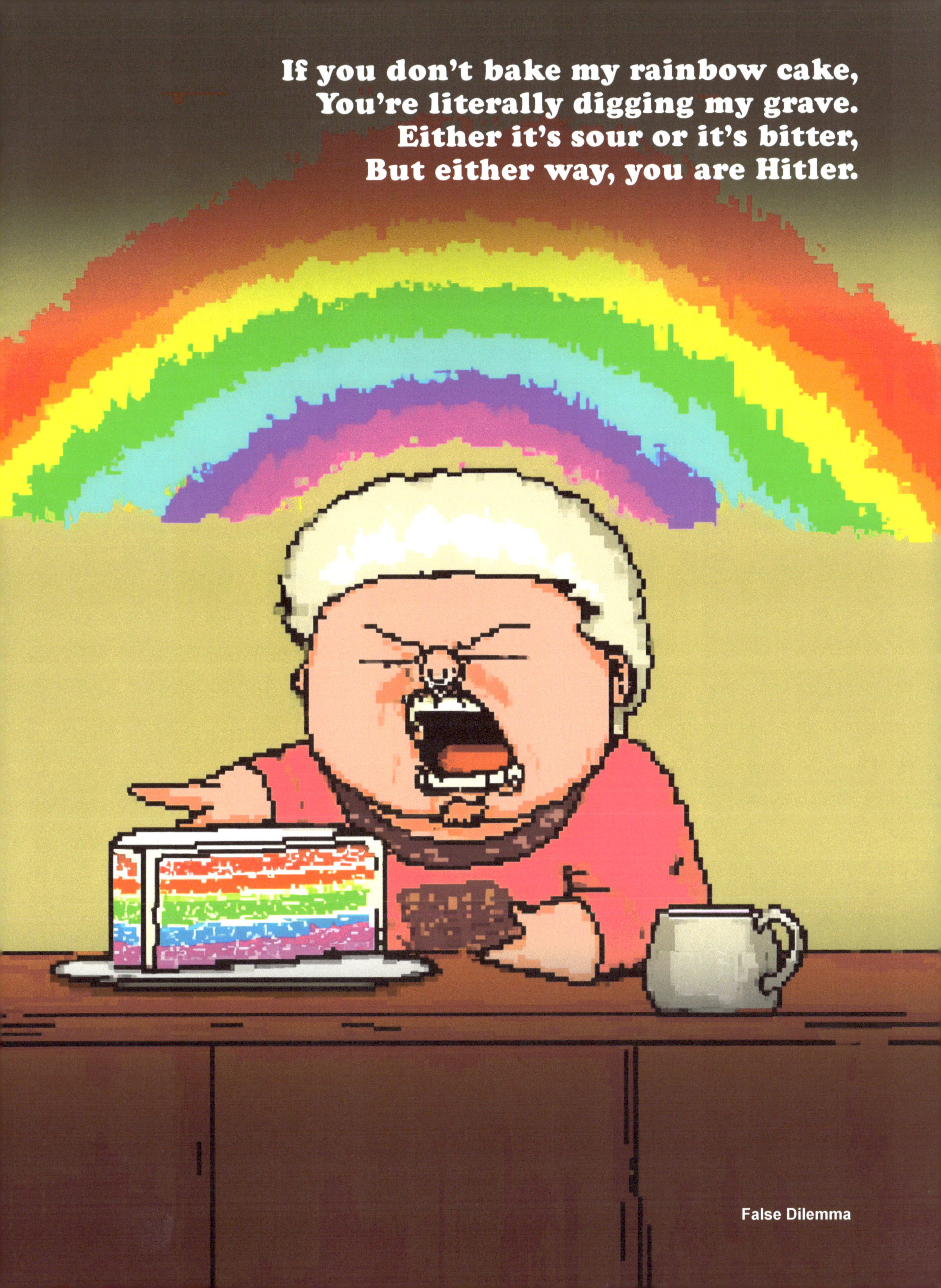
If you don't bake my rainbow cake,
You're literally digging my grave.
Either it's sour or it's bitter,
But either way, you are Hitler.
False Dilemma

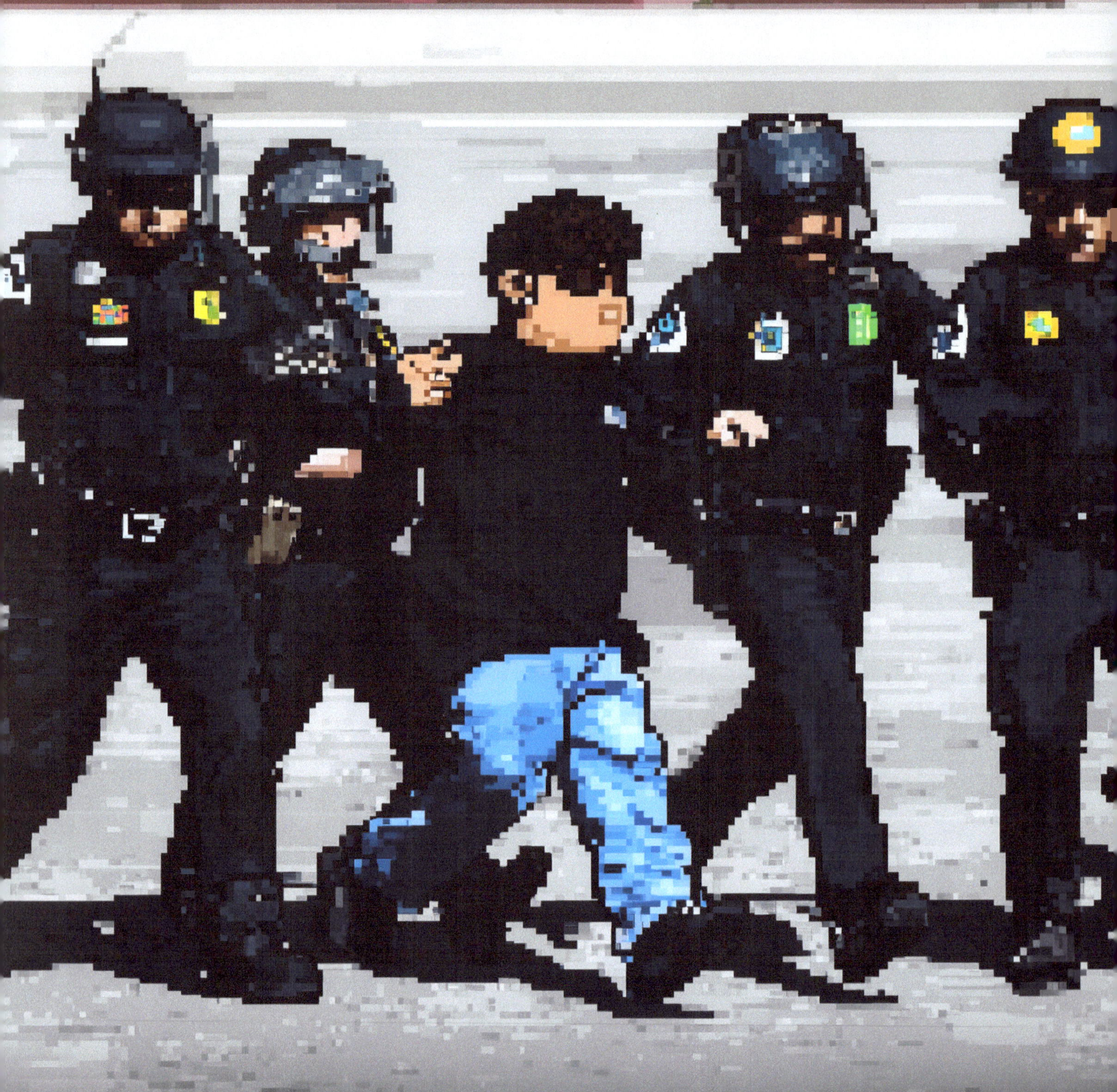

First they deport all of the 'illegals'.
Then they'll imprison all the legal peoples.
They'll put us all in camps much quicker,
With your support you little Hitler.

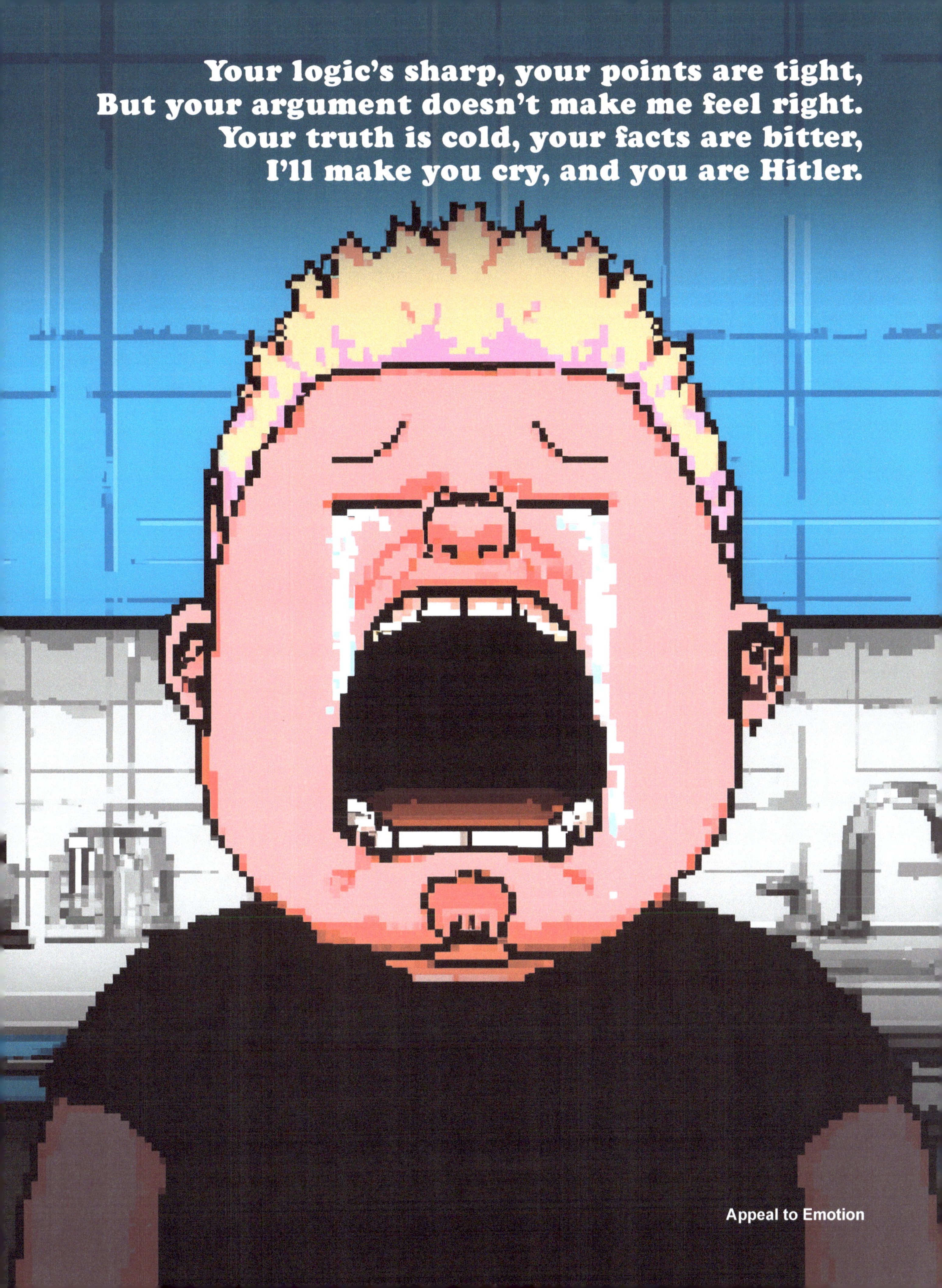
Your logic's sharp, your points are tight,
But your argument doesn't make me feel right.
Your truth is cold, your facts are bitter,
I'll make you cry, and you are Hitler.
Appeal to Emotion

No True Communist Fallacy

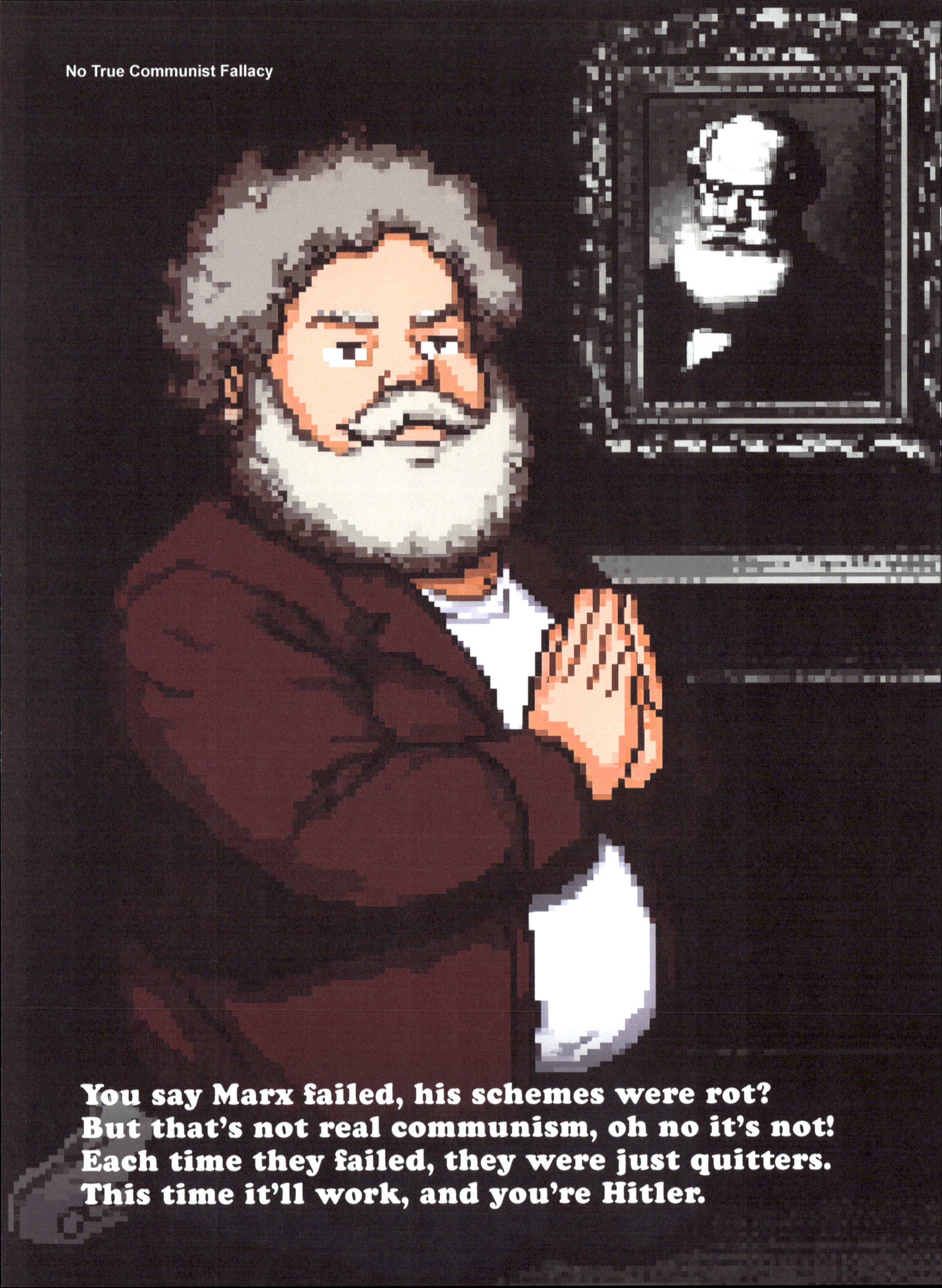

You say Marx failed, his schemes were rot?
But that's not real communism, oh no it's not!
Each time they failed, they were just quitters.
This time it'll work, and you're Hitler.

www.ingramcontent.com/pod-product-compliance
Lightning Source LLC
Chambersburg PA
CBHW041603070526
44586CB00003BA/67